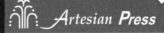

W9-BOM-480

# CHALLENGER

## SANDRA D. BRICKER

Artesian Press
P.O. Box 355 Buena Park, CA 90621

# Take Ten Books
## Disaster

### Other Take Ten Themes:

**Mystery**
**Sports**
**Adventure**
**Chillers**
**Thrillers**
**Romance**
**Horror**
**Fantasy**

Project Editor: Dwayne Epstein
Assistant Editor: Molly Mraz
Graphic Design: Tony Amaro
Cover photo courtesy of NASA
©2003 Artesian Press

*All rights reserved. No part of this publication may be reproduced or transmitted in any form without permission in writing from the publisher. Reproduction of any part of this book, through photocopy, recording, or any electronic or mechanical retrieval system, without the written permission of the publisher is an infringement of copyright law.*

www.artesianpress.com

𝄞 Artesian Press          ISBN 1-58659-021-9

# CONTENTS

# Chapter 1

"I am directing NASA to begin a search in all of our elementary and secondary schools, and to choose as the first citizen passenger in the history of our space program one of America's finest—a teacher . . . When that shuttle lifts off, all of America will be reminded of the crucial role teachers and educators play in the life of our nation. I can't think of a better lesson for our children and our country."

Some said it was nothing more than publicity to gain the support of educators; others said it was just one more thing he would be noted for in the history books. But when President Ronald Reagan made the announcement on August 27, 1984, the whole country took notice.

Average people have been dreaming about space travel for hundreds of years. When Neil Armstrong stepped off the lunar module named Eagle onto the surface of the moon during the Apollo space mission on July 20, 1969, it became that much more attainable.

Science fiction movies, cartoons, television shows, and books have painted wonderful pictures of space travel. Never had it been more real than at that moment in our history—the moment that the President told the entire country that an average citizen would be chosen to ride along on the next space shuttle flight.

The media went wild; all Americans were talking about it. One hundred fourteen nominees were going to be chosen—two from each state, and others from U.S. territories, overseas schools, and the like—and from them, ten semifinalists would be selected. Those ten would undergo medical tests and interviews at the Johnson Space Center. A winner and runner-up would then be chosen.

NASA expected to receive up to 100,000 applications from teachers all across the country, but only about 11,000 submissions were made. Each of the 114 nominees selected underwent a series of interviews, as well as workshops and lectures on space travel. They were given workbooks and videos. They were reminded, maybe for the first time in many years, what it was like to be a student instead of a teacher!

"You will be the 114 most knowledgeable teachers in the country about the space program and how to relate that information to students," Dr. William Pierce told them in his welcoming statement that June.

And he was right. Some of the

teachers involved went back to their hometowns to do wonderful things. Some spoke to the National Commission on Space in Salt Lake City, Utah. Others designed space workshops for their students.

Physical requirements for the Space Participant Program were fairly simple to meet. It involved good eyesight with or without glasses, general good health including blood pressure, and being able to hear a whispered voice at a distance of three feet.

The week of interviews was like the Miss America competitions, but without the swimsuit portion. It was one long talent contest where the teachers were judged on everything from their sense of humor to their imagination.

The people at NASA were interested in finding a candidate who would interview well with the press and look good on the cover of a magazine. They also hoped that the candidate would make creative suggestions on a way to bring "space" back to earth and make the experience real to the rest of the world.

Many of the applicants' ideas were awesome but, in the end, it was the most simple idea that caught their attention: keeping a daily diary.

Every newspaper across the country carried stories about their own local hopefuls. There were two African-Americans who attended the week-long seminar in Washington, D.C.—William M. Dillon, Jr. of San Mateo, California, and Rosa W. Hampston of Christiansted, Virginia. They were featured in a July issue of *Jet*, a magazine devoted to the accomplishments of African-Americans. It was a time when anyone involved with the program could be found on the front page of a newspaper or on the cover of a magazine.

When the time finally came for the

ten finalists to be chosen, NASA put together a special panel of people to make the decision. The panel consisted of celebrities as well as ordinary people. Terri Rosenblatt of the Council of Chief State School Officers was the lucky one to contact the ten finalists.

Those chosen were: Michael Metcalf of Vermont; Dave Marquart of Idaho; Richard Methia of Massachusetts; Peggy Lathlaen of Texas; Barbara Morgan of Idaho; Christa McAuliffe of New Hampshire; Kathleen Beres of Maryland; Niki Wenger of West Virginia; Robert Foerster of Indiana; and Judith Garcia of Virginia.

It was the middle of the night when the phone rang at Christa McAuliffe's home in Concord, New Hampshire, and her husband sleepily answered.

"It's for you," he told his wife. "It's someone from NASA. You made the final ten."

"If you're kidding," she told him,

"you are in big trouble!"

They were the ten happiest teachers in America that week, and they all reported to Houston, Texas, for yet another series of tests and evaluations.

# Chapter 2

The crew for the *Challenger* 10 had been chosen, and they were already training for their mission when the finalists arrived in Houston. The fortunate ones who would fly on the project now known as "Teacher-in-Space" were: Mission Specialist Ellison Onizuka; Payload Specialist Greg Jarvis; Mission Specialist Judy Resnik; Pilot Mike Smith; Mission Specialist Ronald McNair; and Commander Dick Scobee.

At the beginning of his career, Dick Scobee was a test pilot. In many cases, this leads to later becoming an astronaut. He didn't hold out much hope for that because he was so tall and the compartments on the spacecrafts were very small in those days. In 1978, though, he was accepted into astronaut training and six years later, in 1984, served as the pilot on the *Challenger* 5 mission.

He had returned from that flight as excited as a child under his first Christmas tree. "Man was meant to be out there! It's what we have to do," he told his wife, June.

This time, Dick Scobee wasn't just the pilot—he was the commander, the man in charge. He had a first-rate crew, and he was excited to see the mission get underway.

Judy Resnik, one of the mission specialists, had been one of the two astronauts NASA had flown in to talk with the 114 teachers that had assembled in Washington. She told the story of her first flight, when she was one of the first two American women ever in space, back in 1984. That flight had been postponed for two months while repairs were made on the shuttle.

"We take our time because we only have one chance to do it right," she told them.

Commander Scobee was happy to have her on his team, although he was a bit concerned about the civilian who would soon be named to tag along. He was determined to let whomever was chosen know up front that this was no game. He took his job very seriously. He expected everyone around him to do the same.

Although they were enjoying every moment of their new-found stardom, the ten finalists had no choice but to take their jobs as seriously as Scobee did. In Houston, they were put up in a motel near the Space Center and were up each morning before 6:00 a.m.

They were hooked up to machines and they ran treadmills. They rode the "vomit comet," a roller coaster-like device in the shape of a plane which

14

tossed them around in an effort to test them against air sickness. They experienced weightlessness. And they were even zipped inside a dozen or so layers of cloth to find out if they were claustrophobic, or afraid of closed-in spaces.

In addition to all of the physical strain, there was also the added stress of competition. They were making friends with one another, sharing something that millions of Americans would have given almost anything to experience. Yet they could not forget that they were competing against one another for the ultimate honor, the one thing that had brought them all there from their hometowns across the country: Space travel.

"One small step for man. One giant leap for mankind."

Ever since Neil Armstrong uttered those words from the surface of the moon, man has been itching to experience it for himself. Children dream of it, old men write about it, mothers and fathers tell stories about it.

We have traveled into space hundreds of times with the television show, *Star Trek*. Our imaginations have gone wild with the possible creatures we might encounter if we could make the trip ourselves. No other fantasy has been so explored, and yet only a very select few ever get to actually live the dream.

That was why those ten finalists were there. Each one of them carried with them their own childhood hopes and visions of what it would be like, of what they would see, of what they would feel.

In May of 1961, Christa McAuliffe was twelve years old. In the cafeteria of Lincoln Junior High School, she and her classmates sat amazed as they watched the first American-manned space flight on television. Christa excitedly told her friends that she was

16

going to ride in space someday!

Twenty-four years later, she was being tossed about the cabin of a NASA jet bouncing off the walls and turning somersaults in the air. She was preparing for her own chance at making the voyage she'd been dreaming about all those years.

# Chapter 3

When the testing was finally over in Houston, the finalists were sent to Washington, D.C., for the last round of personal interviews. The judges didn't have to think about it for very long. It was, to them, an easy choice.

The teachers waited in Room 7002 at NASA headquarters. The suspense was almost more than they could bear! They'd been through so much, and they were finally going to hear which one of them had been chosen to fly on the *Challenger* with Commander Scobee and his team.

They tried to remain calm, chatting among themselves, tapping the table, biting their nails. Christa McAuliffe and Niki Wenger were making idle conversation about their families and hometowns, trying to pass the time. Christa told Niki that her husband had been the typical single parent lately, and that he had even resorted to eating corn flakes for supper on more than one occasion!

"Excuse me, Christa," said Ann Bradley, the NASA executive who was to break the news they had been waiting for. "But you'd better tell your husband to get a lot more corn flakes! You're the one. You're going up in space!"

The whole room fell silent at that moment. Christa was frozen. It wasn't until one of the teachers, Peggy Lathaen of Texas, ran over to her and gave her a big hug that Christa realized what had just happened. Suddenly, the room was filled with hugs and kisses and chatter and more hugs.

Christa McAuliffe wasn't chosen for

the mission because she was the smartest, or the prettiest, or in the best physical shape. She was chosen for one simple reason: the panel of judges felt that she was spirited and full of wonder. They thought that because of those qualities, she would tell the best story about her experiences when she got back. She was the all-American girl, and NASA hoped that she would become the space program's cheerleader.

The ten finalists went over to the White House that afternoon where Vice President George Bush was planning to make a televised announcement about the outcome to the whole country. Christa had been asked not to tell a soul until after it had been made official. She could hardly wait to call home and tell her husband and two children.

When he introduced Christa as the winner, she timidly shook the Vice

President's hand. She tearfully told the world, "I've made nine wonderful friends over the last two weeks, and when that shuttle goes, there might be one body, but there's going to be ten souls I'm taking with me."

That was the spirit of Christa McAuliffe—the sweetness of her, the cheerleader in her. She was everything NASA hoped she would be, and more. America fell in love with her that day.

Barbara Morgan of Idaho was chosen as Christa's runner-up. If for some reason Christa couldn't fulfill her duties and carry out the mission, Barbara Morgan would step in.

The eight other finalists took vacations from their teaching jobs for a year. They accepted temporary job assignments from NASA while Christa and Barbara were enrolled in pre-flight training school. They took the same training that Payload Specialist Greg Jarvis had taken before being chosen to

*The seven members of the Challenger space shuttle crew are (back, left to right): Ellison Onizuka, Christa McAuliffe, Greg Jarvis, Judy Resnik; (front, left to right) Mike Smith, Dick Scobee, Ron McNair.*

serve on Commander Scobee's team. Like Christa, Greg had been selected, from over six hundred other Hughes Aircraft employees to take a place aboard the shuttle.

Christa and Barbara's training lasted over one hundred hours, all of it having to do with space environment, flight safety, the operation of the shuttle itself, and what each crew member was responsible for. They were students once again instead of teachers. They watched videos, sat in classrooms, or worked on their own.

They even had the chance to fly in a "simulator." It copied the experiences of an actual shuttle flight to test their abilities and see just how they would react in certain situations.

Christa's main purpose on the flight was very simple. She was to make space travel less mysterious, to tell about her experiences in a way that made it real to average people just like her.

In an effort to bring American citizens along on the ride, NASA created the Mission Watch program. Hundreds of schools across the country were hooked up to a satellite, allowing them to watch the shuttle's activities on television as part of their science lessons in school.

A couple of weeks before the launch, the Mission Watch schools were given information packages of charts, schedules, the goals of the mission, and a sort of TV Guide that gave times for watching.

Christa McAuliffe would be teaching students all across the nation by use of the program. Her first lesson was set to be called the "Ultimate Field Trip." She planned to give a tour of the shuttle and show student viewers where the crew would eat, sleep, and exercise, and even how their toilet worked.

Christa's second lesson plan was

called "Where We've Been and Where We're Going." This demonstration was set to include experiments she thought the children of America might find interesting, such as a zero-gravity test, crystal growth formations, and even mixing water and oil in space.

Both of the two lesson plans were scheduled for mid-day during school hours, and they were to last about fifteen minutes each. NASA hoped to include a five-minute question-and-answer period at the end of each session, where children from selected schools could actually communicate with the space shuttle.

There was a chance that Christa's own school could be chosen! Perhaps she would have the opportunity to wave the tiny school flag they had given her before she left for NASA.

Not only were Christa's lessons going to be broadcast live, but the tapes were going to remain on file at NASA as educational tools in the years to come. The Public Broadcasting System (PBS) also planned a documentary about Christa's lessons.

"Everybody can identify with teachers," Christa told *Life* magazine. "We've all had them. I'll be keeping a diary just like some of the women who pioneered the West."

And that's just what Christa McAuliffe was to America: a brave pioneer setting out to go where no average citizen had gone before. Was she scared?

"My only fear," she said during a training session with Commander Scobee at the Space Center, "is that the waste compartment's going to break down."

It wasn't unusual, Christa had been told, for the toilet not to work up there in space!

Christa and Barbara Morgan worked side-by-side like the team that NASA hoped they would be. They shared an office at the center and had their own small apartments in the same building at Peachtree Lane, a nearby complex. They jogged together every day, at least three miles. In spite of the competition that had brought them together, a friendship was forming between them that no one else could ever fully understand.

On their off hours, they would go grocery shopping together or take a dip in the pool. Sometimes they would wander over to the harbor for dinner and talk about their homes, their families, their teaching jobs, and what they missed most.

"I miss my students telling me about their dates," Christa confided in Barbara, and the two shared a laugh.

Neither of them would ever forget their time in Houston, and they made plans to go together on a nation-wide speaking tour after the *Challenger* flight to share all they had learned.

"If the Teacher-in-Space doesn't come back to teach," Christa said, "something's wrong!"

During her pre-flight training, Christa worked with Dick Scobee and Ellison Onizuka to script out the lessons and rehearse what she would say and do once she was in orbit.

"Missions keep going up every month," Commander Scobee said with a smile, "but the Teacher-in-Space is unique. You are the reason we'll be remembered."

That thought remained with her as she finished her training. As the launch day approached, Christa became more and more excited. She could hardly wait to get up into that beautiful blue sky and experience for herself what millions had only been able to dream about.

# Chapter 4

One delay after another held *Challenger* down. Day after day, the mission was postponed. Finally, on January 27, 1986, the weather was more than perfect for a launch and all systems looked like a "Go!" Then a door handle that was there only for the ground crew wouldn't come off the shuttle like it was supposed to.

Someone sent for a screwdriver, but the screw was jammed. Someone else asked for a battery-operated drill, but the battery was dead. Then someone asked for a hacksaw, but none ever arrived. That day of mistakes cost American taxpayers over two hundred thousand dollars and another launch delay.

"I would have gotten the hacksaw sooner," said Ed Corrigan, Christa's father. He watched the action on television in the press room.

Christa's mother playfully offered a woman's perspective. "I would have gotten my nail file."

That night, the temperature dropped down below freezing. Inspection teams were sent to the launch pad during the night, and some concern was raised when they found a great deal of ice there. Later, over two hours were spent repairing a fire detector. The crew was up shortly after 6:00 a.m. with little clue of what had gone on overnight.

On January 28, on her way into the shuttle for yet another try at lift-off, someone brought a shiny red apple and handed it to Christa.

"Save it for me," she said with a grin. "I'll eat it when I get back."

No shuttle had ever been launched in

*Teacher-in-Space Christa McAuliffe, Ellison Onizuka, and Greg Jarvis leave crew headquarters for their trip on the* Challenger *space shuttle.*

weather below fifty-one degrees. But even at that twenty-four-degree temperature, NASA was anxious to break past all the obstacles that had kept *Challenger* grounded and get the shuttle into space.

There was ice on the launch pad, but the winds looked as if they were going to die down. Mission Control agreed to go ahead with the launch.

At just past nine o'clock, the countdown stopped. Someone had spotted ice on the launch pad as they watched the build-up on television and phoned in to tell NASA not to go ahead. An hour later, supervisors decided that the conditions were fine, and the countdown began again.

Engineers were up in arms! Memos had been sent out months before warning NASA of the problems with the "O-rings," those tiny rings responsible for the huge job of sealing in the hot gases in the rocket boosters during a launch. They could fail as a result of freezing temperatures.

Their opinions were tossed back and forth like tennis balls at a match. Those in charge finally made the decision to go ahead despite the warnings of the engineers.

At 11:38 a.m., *Challenger*'s three main engines ignited just as they were supposed to. According to William J. Coughlin, a reporter, there was an especially long moment before the solid rocket boosters kicked into gear. The climb into the morning sky was different than usual.

"This bird is awfully slow in lifting off," he thought. "Normally, shuttles leap like dragons from their lair."

But, in a matter of moments, everything seemed normal again. Mission Control's spokesman, James Wetherbee, could be heard over the speakers as he spoke to the *Challenger* crew.

"Roger, roll, *Challenger*," he said.

Then Commander Scobee responded. After a moment of silence, he also added, ". . .And, Houston, we have roll program."

"*Challenger*, go with throttle up," said Wetherbee.

"Roger, go with throttle up," Scobee replied.

A few seconds later, someone was frantically shouting, "R.T.L.S! R.T.L.S!"

Very few of the spectators recognized the code, which meant, "Return to launch site."

Seventy-three seconds into the launch, a spectacular orange light filled the sky, followed by a tail of white smoke. It was an eerie, soundless fireworks display. All of the world fell silent beneath quiet gasps and barely heard moans and sobs. It just couldn't be! The *Challenger* had exploded.

Americans went into shock at 11:39 a.m. on January 28, 1986. The Teacher-in-Space they had come to love, the crew they knew so well through the media, the beginning of an era of space travel that lived up to the hopes painted by dreamers for decades . . . all of it was gone!

NASA had announced plans to send a journalist into space next, followed by an artist, a novelist, maybe even a factory worker in space. Christa was to be the leader in a long line of "ordinary folks" to experience space travel. But on the 28th anniversary of the first American satellite sent into space, a service was held at Johnson Space Center honoring the late crew of the *Challenger*.

"Sometimes when we reach for the stars," President Reagan said that day, "we fall short. But we must pick ourselves up again and press on, despite the pain."

Earlier, the President met with the families and friends of the *Challenger* crew and offered whatever comfort he could to a grieving, confused group of people.

"I wish there was something I could say to make it easier," he told them, "but there just aren't any words. We sorrow more for ourselves and in the fact that we will miss them. This should be tempered by the joy that they are receiving the blessings God reserved for them. We shall all see them together again."

# Chapter 5

"Good morning, Christa," said Mission Control that fateful morning as they tested her headset. "Hope we go today."

"Good morning," she replied in that sweet way of hers. "Hope so, too."

No one knew those would be her last words.

Human error had taken the lives of Christa, Greg Jarvis, and those five dedicated astronauts of the *Challenger* crew. Barbara Morgan, second in line for the shuttle, could only stand in the bleachers, shivering in the cold, watching.

The wish that she was in Christa's place was still fresh in her mind at the time that the O-rings failed and the shuttle exploded. Ironically, Barbara escaped death by a narrow margin that day. Yet she felt it as strongly as if she had been aboard.

NASA quickly gathered all videos of the disaster that very day. Reporters were asked to turn over their notes. Cameramen handed in their equipment. NASA conducted its own investigation of the accident using every possible shred of evidence they could find to reconstruct the launch.

Several video accounts, when put together, captured a series of puffs of smoke that led the experts to the origin of the trouble. The O-rings had failed to do their job. The O-rings were the little rubber rings that hold in the hot gases in the rocket boosters during the launch. The cold weather had caused them to let go, just as someone had warned months before the launch.

The investigators were able to piece

together most of what must have happened inside the *Challenger* during those horrible seconds leading up to the explosion. From the ground, everything seemed pretty normal. Maybe a little slower, a little shakier. It wasn't until the tapes were analyzed that three bright flashes were noticed, the final one turning into the explosion that shocked the world.

At least some of the crew, the investigators reported, probably survived the explosions and were using the air systems that were in place behind their seats, much like the oxygen masks on board an airline flight. It is thought that some members of the crew were aware of what was happening even as the broken shuttle dropped downward. The warning lights on the instrument panel probably flashed before them, and the blinding light of the fire most likely glared at them through the windows.

The shuttle pilot, Michael Smith, was the last to be heard on NASA's communication system. He simply muttered, "Uh-oh."

Immediately afterward, Dick Scobee had flipped on his own microphone and was prepared to speak into it. NASA lost touch with them before Scobee could be heard.

The crew cabin fell toward the ocean at nearly 2,000 miles per hour—over 35 times the speed of an automobile on a fast-moving freeway. Because of the high rate of speed, the crew members that had survived the explosion were probably unconscious by the time the cabin hit the water.

Over a month after the explosion, the crew's remains were found when the cabin was recovered from the Atlantic Ocean, and their families were reminded of the disaster all over again.

In the months following the tragedy, the seven families came together to

*The space shuttle* Challenger *can be seen over the Kennedy Space Center after the explosion.*

build plans for the *Challenger* Space Centers. These centers would educate children about space travel by using simulators, much like the one Christa trained on for her mission into space. One center is now open in Houston, with others in the planning and fundraising stages.

"We've formed a family of our own," June Scobee, wife of Commander Dick Scobee said. "When my children come, or when Steven McAuliffe [Christa's husband] brings his children, this house just lights up with the laughter. For the first time, too, I'm making really deep, committed friendships."

After the explosion of the *Challenger*, NASA promised the American public that they would correct all the problems and be back in the business of space travel within a year. But that was one promise they would not be able to keep.

Nearly two and a half years later, on

September 29, 1989, the next mission was launched. Over two hundred changes had been made before Discovery ever left the launch pad.

The world held its breath that day. Five astronauts were on board, and they performed routine tasks during their four days in orbit—at least as "routine" as things can be 184 miles out in space! A communications satellite was released, and a few tests were performed. No one wanted to think it could happen again, and yet people couldn't keep the thought from their minds.

# Chapter 6

The spirit of the *Challenger* crew lives on through their loved ones. The pilot, Michael Smith, stands out in the mind of his wife Jane as "a very, very special person." Not because of his contributions to American history, or because he was the last one to be heard aboard the shuttle. What she remembers is the love he had for his family.

"When I was pregnant with our first child," she recalled, "he had his sister-in-law teach him to sew so he could make me a maternity dress. It was a green corduroy jumper, and it lasted through three pregnancies! I loved that dress; I just couldn't throw it away.

"All the children's bedroom furniture

was also designed and built by Mike, and whenever our children were away, Mike helped them maintain their lawn-mowing business in Houston. Our friends used to say, 'It's so funny to look out and see an astronaut mowing our lawn!'"

It seems that the *Challenger* crew members were remembered for their spirits more than anything else.

"One evening, I visited him at the Massachusetts Institute of Technology (M.I.T.) where he was working on his Ph.D.," said Cheryl McNair. She was the wife of Ronald McNair, Mission Specialist on the *Challenger* flight. "After he finished his lab work, he packed his books and data into a duffel bag, and we walked to his car near the river. He put the bag down by the car door, and we walked the short distance down to the river to see the lights reflected in it. When we got back to the car, the bag was gone. The material in it represented years of work!"

Cheryl couldn't believe Ron's reaction. "He just looked at me calmly and said, 'I have some results in notebooks at home and at the lab. What I don't have, well, I'll have to duplicate.' He was silent for a while, but he wasn't outraged or depressed. He was going to solve this problem without showing strain. After that, he worked day and night in the lab for about four months. The result was that the deadline for his doctoral thesis was reached, and the professor thought the paper turned out quite well—even improved!"

Greg Jarvis' wife, Marcia, remembers her husband as someone who always finished what he started.

"He was an avid squash player," she said. "He entered his first tournament as a novice. At one point, the other player swung his racket and hit Greg just below the eye. He needed stitches, so he hopped on his motorcycle and went to the hospital. The doctor, who was a friend, stitched him up, and Greg raced back to the tournament. He didn't win, but he finished the game!"

"Our family always tried to be together for dinner," said June Scobee, wife of Commander Dick Scobee. "And Dick listened as closely to our daily adventures as we did to his. Just hours after Dick's first space flight, we went to our favorite restaurant, and Dick explained with marvelous detail the visual images and colors and light he had seen.

"As we talked, he kept bringing his silverware and napkin very close to his plate. Then he stuck his napkin under his plate. I finally asked what he was doing, and he said, 'Oh, I was afraid my napkin might float away!'"

Much like his crewmate Christa McAuliffe, Ellison Onizuka is remembered by his wife, Lorna, as someone with a very strong sense of love toward the children of his country.

"That's the part I admired most," she said. "When children asked Ellison what space meant to him, he'd say that in his earlier years, he thought space was just the volume between his ears!"

On a more serious note, Ellison's wife describes him this way: "The enthusiasm for space exploration was his gift to these young people. He encouraged the freedom to dream and the commitment to making those dreams come true. He always said there was nothing wrong with dreams. They were reachable! They were tomorrow's reality."

Judith Resnik felt much the same way.

"Judith once wrote a letter to a friend," her father, Marvin Resnik, said, "in which she told her that nothing is obtained by wishing for it. Hard work and perseverance are necessary for success. And that's the way she lived her life."

It was the way all of the members of the *Challenger* crew lived their lives. They worked hard, and the only thing they seemed to love more than their work was their families—the families they lived with and their extended families across the United States, the ones dreaming the dreams along with them.

And those dreams are, in a small way, being realized by the *Challenger* Space Centers. They teach the children of America to continue reaching out for those stars that have fascinated us since the dawn of time.

"Man was meant to be out there. It's what we have to do."

—Dick Scobee

# Bibliography

"The Crew of Challenger 51-L." *Space World* March 1986.

Fichter, George. *The Space Shuttle.* New York: F. Watts, 1990.

Hohler, Robert T. *I Touched the Future: The Story of Christa McAuliffe.* New York: Random House, 1986.

"NASA Classes Start for Ten Teachers in a Race to Space." *People* 29 July 1985.

"Reach for the Stars: Reagan Leads U.S. in Bidding Crew Farewell." *Los Angeles Times* 1 February 1986.

"Remembering Judy." *Ms.* June 1986.

"The Space Flight Bandwagon." *Space World* December 1985.

"The Space Teacher." *Life* March 1986.

"A Teacher Crams for a Classroom
in Orbit." *Life* December 1985.

"Teachers in Space." *Sky & Telescope*
February 1985.

"A Thousand Days of Tears." *Ladies
Home Journal* February 1989.

"Tribute." *People* 22 December 1986.

"Two Blacks Among Teachers Vying for
Shuttle Flight." *Jet* 22 July 1985.